Presented to:

_____

From:

_____

Psalm 127:3

ZONDERVAN°

You're the Best Dad

Copyright © 2014 by Zondervan

Requests for information should be addressed to:

Zondervan, *Grand Rapids, Michigan* 49530

ISBN 978-0-310-33990-8

Cover design: Milkglass Creative, LLC
Cover illustration: Milkglass Creative, LLC
Interior design: Mallory Perkins
Stock images p#/artist © Shutterstock: 1, 3, 6, 7, 16, 17, 50, 51/campincool, 24, 25/wawritto

Printed in China

14 15 16 17 18 19 20 /Tims/ 22 21 20 19 18 17 16 15 14 13 12 11 10 9 8 7 6 5 4 3 2 1

TABLE OF CONTENTS

Parents are the pride of their children.
Proverbs 17:6

WHEN DAD WAS A KID . . .

His favorite TV show was

_____.

His favorite food was

_____.

The chore he hated most was

_____.

His favorite hobby was

_____.

Dad had a pet that was a:

a. dog   c. fish

b. cat   d. rock

DAD'S FAVORITES

Dad's favorite color is

_____.

Dad's favorite song is

_____.

Dad's favorite food is

_____.

Dad's favorite restaurant is

_____.

Dad's favorite game to play is

_____.

DAD AT WORK

What kind of job does Dad have?

_____

What does Dad do when he is at work?

_____

If you went to work with Dad for a day,
how would you help him do his job?

_____

Draw a picture of you and Dad at work together!

A DAY IN THE LIFE OF DAD

Fill in Dad's calendar with what
he does on a typical day.

What time does Dad . . .

wake up? _____

make breakfast? _____

go to work? _____

eat lunch? _____

come home from work? _____

play with me after dinner? _____

go to bed? _____

DAD ESSENTIALS

What is Dad's name?

_____

How old is Dad?

_____

How tall is Dad?

_____

How much does Dad weigh?

_____

What color are Dad's eyes?

_____

What color is Dad's hair?

_____

Draw a picture of what Dad looks like!

Do you and Dad share any interests?
Check all of the things you both enjoy!

- ☐ reading books
- ☐ playing sports
- ☐ working with tools
- ☐ cooking
- ☐ watching movies
- ☐ listening to music

DAD AS A SUPERHERO

If your dad really did have a superpower, what would it be?

_____

Who would his sidekick be?

_____

How would your dad and his sidekick save the world?

_____

_____

_____

_____

_____

Draw a picture of Dad and his sidekick in their superhero costumes!

Listen, my sons, to a father's instruction;
pay attention and gain understanding.
Proverbs 4:1

SCHOOL DAYS

What is the name of your school?

_____

What are you favorite subjects in school?

_____

Who is your favorite teacher?

_____

What is in your favorite school lunch?

_____

In one word, tell Dad about your day at school.

_____

Draw a picture of how you get to school!
Do you walk, ride in a car, or take the bus?

PLAYGROUND FUN

What is your favorite thing to do on the playground or at the park?

_____

What do you think Dad would like to do most at the playground or park? Why?

_____

Check all the things your dad can do:

- ☐ Jump higher than a building
- ☐ Catch a ball
- ☐ Throw a football over a mountain
- ☐ Climb to the top of the jungle gym
- ☐ Swing higher than the top of the swing set
- ☐ Slide down the slide
- ☐ Dunk a basketball
- ☐ Win a foot race
- ☐ Jump 100 times over the jump rope without tripping
- ☐ Win a game of tag
- ☐ Hit a home run
- ☐ See-saw with me
- ☐ Swing all the way across the monkey bars

THIS OR THAT?

Circle the one Dad would choose:

Chocolate or vanilla?   Tea or cola?

Sleeping in late or waking up early?

Dogs or cats?   Cake or pie?

Playing outside or reading a book?

Spiders or worms?   Hamburger or hotdog?

The beach or the mountains?

Fold laundry or wash dishes?

TV shows or movies?   Cook or get takeout?

Mow the lawn or take out the garbage?

ANIMAL ANTICS

If Dad were an animal, what animal would he be? Why?

_____

What animal would you be? Why?

_____

What is your favorite animal?

_____

What is Dad's favorite animal?

_____

Draw your dad's favorite animal!

IN THE KITCHEN WITH DAD

My favorite dish Dad makes is

_____.

My dad makes the best

_____ in the whole world.

I like it when Dad makes

_____ for breakfast.

I like it when Dad makes

_____ for dinner.

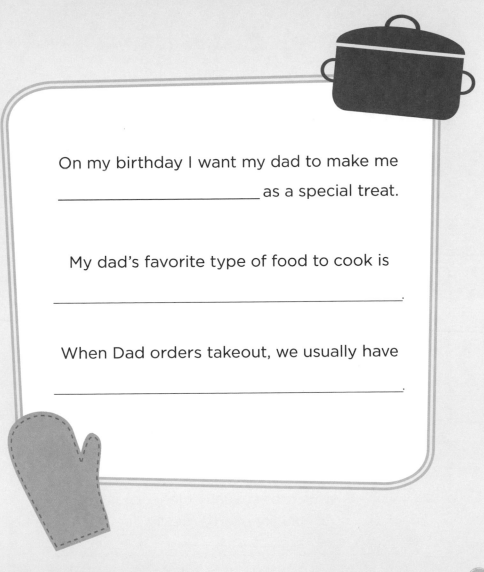

On my birthday I want my dad to make me

_____ as a special treat.

My dad's favorite type of food to cook is

_____.

When Dad orders takeout, we usually have

_____.

OUR FAMILY HOME

Which state do you live in?

_____

What is the name of the town where you live?

_____

What is your favorite room in your house?

_____

What color is your room?

_____

Do you have your own room, or do
you share it with someone?

_____

Is your room usually clean, or is
it usually pretty messy?

_____

Draw a picture of you and your
dad in front of your house!

DAD ON SUNDAY

The name of my church is

_____.

I like to sing this song with Dad:

_____.

Dad usually wears _____ to church.

My dad's favorite Bible story is

_____.

Dad's favorite place to eat after church is

_____.

When it comes to arriving at church, my dad typically:

a. gets to church pretty early
b. arrives right on time for church
c. can be a little late sometimes

Dad is most likely to do which one of these things at church?

a. Sing in the choir
b. Greet visitors
c. Lead a prayer
d. Teach Sunday school

Fill the speech bubbles with things
that Dad says the most.

My favorite thing that Dad says is

_____.

PICTURE PERFECT

Attach a photo of your dad to this page,
and draw a picture frame around it.

AT THE MOMENT

	Today	When Dad was my age
How much is a can of soda?	_____	_____
Who is the president?	_____	_____
Who is the biggest pop star?	_____	_____
What is the most popular cartoon on TV?	_____	_____

WHEN I GROW UP . . .

I want to live _____.

I want to go to college at _____.

I want to be a _____.

My first job will pay $ _____ a year.

I will go on vacation to _____.

DAD IS BETTER AT . . .

Do you think your dad would be better
at painting a picture, building a birdhouse,
or running a race? Why?

_____.

_____.

_____.

_____.

_____.

_____.

_____.

_____.

Do you think your dad would be better at: (circle one on each line)

a. being a waiter

b. being president of the United States

a. being a famous painter

b. being a construction worker

a. cooking a Thanksgiving meal

b. eating a Thanksgiving meal

a. running a science lab

b. running a day care

a. growing flowers

b. growing rocks

a. being a football player

b. being a baseball player

a. surfing a huge ocean wave

b. snowboarding down a mountain

a. walking on dinosaur feet

b. walking on caterpillar feet

a. milking a cow

b. herding sheep

a. kicking a field goal

b. dancing in *The Nutcracker*

MY FUNNY DAD

The most embarrassing thing Dad
has ever done to me is

_____.

My dad thinks he is funny when he

_____.

I think Dad is funny when he

_____.

Dad's favorite joke is

_____.

What's the funniest April Fool's joke
Dad has ever played on you?

_____

MY DAD DOES GREAT THINGS

What is the nicest thing Dad has ever done for you?

_____

What is the kindest thing you've seen
Dad do for someone else?

_____

What is the coolest thing Dad has ever said to you?

_____

Draw a picture of the time your
dad helped you the most!

OH SO HANDSOME!

Help Dad see what he looks like by drawing the parts of his ruggedly handsome face!

Dad's hair looks like this:

Dad's eyes look like this:

Dad's nose looks like this:

Dad's ears look like this:

Dad's smile looks like this:

Do you look like your dad? Check all
of the features you both share!

☐ eye color
☐ nose shape
☐ hair color
☐ ear shape
☐ smile

PARTY PLANNER

When is Dad's birthday?

_____

What is Dad's favorite gift you've ever given to him?

_____

If you could give Dad anything, what gift would you give him?

_____

What is Dad's favorite birthday tradition?

_____

Draw a birthday cake for Dad, and decorate it with his favorite things!

MEDIA DAD

Reading

When we read together, Dad and I like to read:

a. picture books   c. magazines

b. my Bible   d. websites

Our favorite book is about _____.

When I read my Bible, I like to read about _____.

Music

Dad's favorite type of music is _____.

His favorite radio station is _____.

Dad's favorite song is _____.

Dad's favorite band is _____.

When Dad dances and sings, I think he is:

a. good
b. really good
c. a real star
d. well . . . he might need a few pointers from me

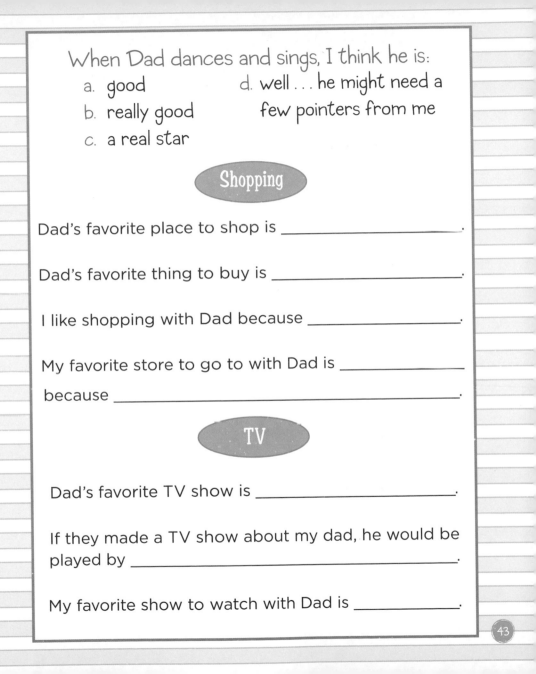

Shopping

Dad's favorite place to shop is _____.

Dad's favorite thing to buy is _____.

I like shopping with Dad because _____.

My favorite store to go to with Dad is _____

because _____.

TV

Dad's favorite TV show is _____.

If they made a TV show about my dad, he would be played by _____.

My favorite show to watch with Dad is _____.

43

DAD ON THE FARM

What are Dad's favorite vegetables?

_____

If Dad were a farmer, which plants would he grow?

_____

If Dad were a farmer, I think
he would definitely have:

a. horses   d. sheep
b. chickens   e. pigs
c. cows

If Dad were a barnyard animal, I think he would be a

_____.

My favorite farm animal is

_____.

If I were a farmer, I would plant

_____.

I think my dad would be a great farmer because he

_____.

Draw a picture of your dad dressed like a farmer!

DAD'S TOOLBOX

Dad's favorite tool is

_____

Try to draw your dad's toolbox!

LESSONS FROM DAD

What is something that Dad is great at doing?

_____

What is your favorite thing that
Dad has taught you to do?

_____

What three things do you want
Dad to teach you to do?

1. _____

2. _____

3. _____

DAD IS MY FAVORITE!

Attach your favorite picture of your
dad. Why is it your favorite?

_____

_____

_____

_____

Attach your favorite picture of you and your dad together. Why is this picture special to you?

_____

_____

_____

_____

[Love] always protects, always trusts, always hopes, always perseveres.
1 Corinthians 13:7

VACATION

I think Dad would rather go to:
(circle one on each line)

a. Disney World   b. Yankee Stadium

a. the Grand Canyon   b. the Mall of America

a. Las Vegas   b. Delaware

a. Hawaii   b. Alaska

a. Chuck E. Cheese's   b. McDonald's

When we're on vacation, my
dad would like to stay in:

a. a hotel   b. a camping tent

My dad's favorite vacation we've ever taken is

_____.

My dad's favorite thing do to on vacation is

_____.

On vacation, my dad would rather:
a. kick back and relax   b. plan tons of activities
for us to do

Sometimes, Dad and I go out just him
and me. I like it when we go to

_____.

If I had the whole day to spend with
Dad, I would want us to

_____.

The best day I ever spent with Dad was when we

_____

_____

_____.

FANCY FUN

Have you and Dad ever been to a:
- ☐ birthday party
- ☐ wedding
- ☐ Christmas party

Do you ever have to dress up for special days?

_____

If you could take your dad somewhere fancy,
where would you take him? Why?

_____

_____

_____

_____

_____

Draw what Dad looks like when he dresses up!

OUT AND ABOUT

My dad and I like to:

☐ go to the movies
☐ go shopping at the mall
☐ go to the library

If my dad had a day to himself, I think he would go to

_____.

When I'm in school, I secretly think my dad goes to

_____.

When Dad takes me shopping, I'm:

    a. super excited!
    b. so bored
    c. hoping we can get to the toy aisle!

Draw a picture of the face you make
while shopping with Dad!

HAPPY HOLIDAYS

Dad's favorite holiday is

_____.

He likes it because

_____.

My favorite thing about spending
holidays with Dad is

_____.

My favorite holiday tradition
with Dad is when we

_____.

Dad's favorite holiday tradition is when we

_____.

The best present my dad ever
gave me for a holiday was

_____.

The worst present my dad ever
gave me for a holiday was

_____.

The best present I ever gave my
dad for a holiday was

_____.

I like it when Dad decorates the house for

_____ because

_____.

CHRISTMAS CHEER!

My dad's favorite Christmas song is

_____.

My favorite Christmas ornament is

_____.

My favorite Christmas song is

_____.

My favorite Christmas snack is

_____.

The best Christmas memory I
have with Dad is when

_____.

My dad's favorite Christmas movie is

_____.

My favorite Christmas movie is

_____.

Attach or draw your favorite picture of
you and your dad at the holidays.

BIRTHDAY FACES

At the bottom of the page, attach a photo of your dad from one of his birthday parties. On the opposite page, attach a picture of yourself from your birthday party at the same age. What similarities and differences do you see in the pictures?

Honor your father and your mother, as the Lord your God has commanded you.

—Deuteronomy 5:16

ABOUT THE AUTHOR

NAME

_____

AGE

_____

DATE

_____

Dad, I think you are the best because

_____.